My First Latino Monologue Book

A SENSE OF CHARACTER

MY FIRST ACTING SERIES: VOLUME 6

SMITH AND KRAUS

MY FIRST ACTING SERIES

This groundbreaking new series is for truly young actors—monologues, scenes, and technique book for the elementary school set. Each book builds on the one before it, so skills grow as students grow. This material is comprehensible, relatable, and fun!

My First Monologue Book: 100 Monologues for Young Children

My Second Monologue Book: Famous and Historical People, 101 Monologues for Young Children

My Third Monologue Book: Places Near and Far, 102 Monologues for Young Children

My First Scene Book: 51 One-Minute Scenes about Etiquette

My Second Scene Book: 52 Two-Minute Scenes about Imaginary People and Places

My First Latino Monologue Book: A Sense of Character, 100 Monologues for Young Children

My Second Latino Monologue Book: A Sense of Place, 100 Monologues for Young Children

My Third Latino Monologue Book: Finding Your Voice!, 100 Monologues for Young Children

My First Latino Scene Book: 51 One-Minute Scenes about Friends

My Second Latino Scene Book: 52 Two-Minute Scenes about Family

My Teacher's First Acting Technique Book:
Opening the Stage Door for Kids K–3

My Teacher's First Acting Series Guide
with lesson plans, games, and interactive exercises

My First **Latino** Monologue Book

A SENSE OF CHARACTER

100 Monologues for Young Children

MY FIRST ACTING SERIES: VOLUME 6

A SMITH AND KRAUS BOOK • HANOVER, NEW HAMPSHIRE

A Smith and Kraus Book
Published by Smith and Kraus, Inc.
177 Lyme Road, Hanover, NH 03755
www.SmithandKraus.com

First Edition: July 2008
Manufactured in the United States of America
9 8 7 6 5 4 3 2 1

Illustrations by Mayleen Ramirez

ISBN-13: 978-1-57525-607-8 / ISBN-10 1-57525-607-X
Library of Congress Control Number: 2008927859

Contents

Introduction

Hey!

Welcome to the brand-spankin' new *My First Latino Monologue Book*.

This is the first in a series of several monologue and scene books written just for you, young actors who might speak more than one language, who might have a last name like Dominguez or Fernandez or Salzedo, and who might have never seen a monologue about an *abuelo* or *abuela* before.

These monologues are an average of a minute long. Some of the monologues are longer. Some are shorter. Feel free to make cuts if you need to—that means cut some lines out if you need a shorter monologue.

Some have some Spanish words in them, but some don't. Don't be afraid to challenge yourself! If there's a word you don't know how to pronounce perfectly, ask Mom or Dad or Abuelo or Tio Whatever, or ask a Spanish teacher at school.

This book is about people you know, like the hairdresser, the cop on the corner, or a boring teacher at school. And people you probably don't know: an astronaut, a mad scientist—even a witch! You get to pretend to be those people, which means thinking about how they move and how they talk, what they are wearing and what their favorite food is. Each monologue is followed by an imagination or hidden-clue question to get you thinking in-depth about the character.

Take a look, enjoy, explore, and—most importantly?

Be yourself.

I'm out.

—M. Ramirez

50 Monologues for Boys

ALBERTO THE CONSTRUCTION WORKER

Alberto is very friendly. He holds a lunch box.

I've been workin' on this building for three months, man. I hang off the end and I wear a big hard-hat 'cause you never know what's gonna fall on your head.

My friend Vinnie had a hammer fall on his head last year, now he can't whistle anymore. It's true, I promise you, man.

Yeah. Construction workin' is the only thing I've ever known, but you know what? I love it, and it's not hard to understand why.

I see people in suits with fancy briefcases, man. They always look like they'd rather be somewhere else, but not me. When I'm dangling off the thirty-second floor having a hotdog with Vinnie . . . man . . . I know I love my job.

An Imagination Question for the Actor

What do you imagine Alberto has in his pockets?

ALEJANDRO THE VIOLINIST

Alejandro is very proper. Maybe he wears a tuxedo. Maybe he holds a violin.

It's not easy playing any instrument. But this one, well, it's probably the hardest in the world. That's what my teacher says, at least. I've been playing since I was four years old. Four. Let's just say it's been a VERY HARD two years. I go to practice and practice standing straight, and I do drills, and I have to wear a fancy tuxedo when I play concerts.

Not "recitals." No. My mom says, "Recitals are for regular players." Not me. I play concerts. There's a difference, she says. Though, to me, the only difference is that I gotta wear a tux.

The sound of a violin is different. My teacher says it's the sound that angels probably make when they cry. I dunno if that's true, but sometimes when I play alone—sometimes I make myself cry. Not 'cause I'm good . . . but 'cause what I really wanna do is play the drums.

Imagination Questions for the Actor

What's Alejandro's posture like?

Does he like playing the violin?

ANDRES THE LAWYER GUY

Andres is a serious businessman in a suit. He checks his watch.

I have a lot of cases. And not just legal, law cases. I have briefcases and suitcases. I wear shiny shoes and I talk on my cell phone a whole lot. I have fancy lunches with the people I work with, and I know how to make thirteen types of tie-knots . . . but my job isn't just "lawyer."

I help people. Every day. People make fun of us a whole lot, but really, I do. You'd be surprised how many people don't know the rules, the laws, the EVERYTHING, and that's really what my job is.

I fight for people who might be in trouble, who might be innocent.

It's a lot more than fancy lunches and tie-knots.

An Imagination Question for the Actor

What kind of tie do you think Andres is wearing?

ARTURITO THE DINOSAUR

Arturito the Dinosaur has his hands close to his sides, like a T-Rex.

It's not easy being extinct. Oh, how I miss the old days. We didn't have TV or video games or airplanes or any of that. All we did for fun was chase around helpless little dinosaurs for days. It was great. Hilarious fun.

And then, when we were good and ready, we made the helpless little dinosaurs our lunch.

It was fantastic.

Now what do I have? Now if I want to have good conversation, I have to go into a fancy museum and talk to my cousin Harvey's bones . . . That's not funny, don't laugh. You think about talking to your cousin Harvey the T-Rex's bones.

It's horrible. Some of them aren't even his bones. They piece those things together from across the world. Two of his ribs just don't fit right. Trust me, he was my T-Rex cousin.

An Imagination Question for the Actor

How do you think a T-Rex would walk?

CARLOS THE SUPER

> *"Super" is short for superintendent. That's the guy you call when you have problems with stuff in your apartment, like the faucet starts dripping or the heater doesn't work.*

My job isn't as easy as it looks. It's always something. If it's not a heater, it's a sink. If it's not a sink, it's an oven or a fire alarm . . . Oh no, the phone is ringing. It's Mrs. McCloskey, an annoying lady who lives in my building.

(He picks up the phone.) Mrs. McCloskey, I'll fix it tomorrow. I got tickets to the football game. I gotta go, it's the finals. OK? Bye, Mrs. McCloskey. *(He hangs up.)*

Jeez Louise. That lady . . . She's crazy. She's got seventeen cats and she complains about her drains getting clogged with cat hair. LADY, your drain's getting clogged with cat hair 'cause you've got SEVENTEEN of the crazy things. Get GOLDFISH. Goldfish won't clog the drains unless you try to get rid of 'em all at once. She's lucky I don't report her to the Crazy Police or something.

A Hidden-Clue Question for the Actor

What do you think Carlos does when he's not working?

CESAR THE FIREFIGHTER

Cesar stands holding a kitten. He wears a fireman's helmet. He talks to someone.

Sir, you've gotta stop calling us to get your cat outta the tree.

I know you love your kitty very much, but this is the tenth time you've called, and, you gotta trust me, the fire department has a lot more important stuff to be worrying about, OK? Like burning houses. Like fires. Those are pretty important to us . . . We're the FIRE department. Not the cat-saving-call-us-'cause-we've-got-that-big-ladder department. OK?

I know it's a pretty awesome ladder thing, and I know it can go like at least forty feet in the air, and I know that's really cool, but well, what's the difference between you calling us to save your cat and Mrs. Hammond calling us to paint the top floor of her house?

We're not the we'll-paint-the-top-floor-of-your-house department, either.

A Hidden-Clue Question for the Actor

How many times has Cesar saved this cat?

CHINO THE BASEBALL PLAYER

Chino is a very famous baseball player. He's signing autographs after a big game. He has his baseball mitt in one hand.

Yeah, when we were in the middle of the seventh inning, that's when coach said, "Chino, it's time to bring out your pitch *secreto,* and I knew what that meant. We've been working on it in practice. I call it *secreto* because that means "secret." I mean, I guess that's pretty obvious probably, but in case you didn't know, that's the name of that pitch. You wanna picture? Sure. *(He poses for a picture.)*

I never dreamed I'd be here, you know. Growing up in the Dominican Republic, my brothers and I didn't even have baseball mitts. We used my mom's old oven mitts, and we used to catch like that. And now, look at me, man. Another picture? Sure. Yeah, I can sign your ball. *(He signs a baseball.)*

Hey, you know what? *(He tosses the mitt.)* I got a couple of those now. That one's for you, buddy. Our "*secreto.*"

A Hidden-Clue Question for the Actor

What position does Chino play?

DAVID THE CABLE GUY

David has a bunch of tools and cables popping out of his pockets. He's leaving a house, talking to the owner.

OK, I think that's about it, Mr. Hernandez. You got a basic cable setup. I installed Package One. That means you get the News Channel, Mundo Latino, SportsChannel One and Two, but not Three, you get Cartoon Extravaganza and AnimalWorld Supreme, but you don't get SuperMovie Channel.

If you wanna get SuperMovie Channel, you've gotta get Premium Package Thirteen. Then you'll also get Mundo Latino, SportsChannel One, Two, Three, Four. You won't get Cartoon Extravaganza, but you WILL get SportsChannel 3-D.

Call the company. They'll set you up.

It's pretty cool, it's like footballs are flying at your face. I gotta get back to the truck. Bye.

An Imagination Question for the Actor

What other kind of stuff does David have in his truck?

DR. DIEGO THE MAD SCIENTIST

Diego wears a lab coat and has crazy hair. He works on crazy experiments. He holds two beakers, each half-filled with liquid.

FINALLY, Pedro . . . Our experiments are complete. All my calculations should be correct. Tonight, it happens! TONIGHT!

The world will finally really see me for what I am not a crazy mad scientist, but a genius, a real-life, misunderstood GENIUS! All I have to do is mix THIS, Potion ONE, with my newest creation and concoction, Potion TWO . . . and finally, my mystical but incredibly scientific SUPERFORMULA will be COMPLETE! TONIGHT! It happens TONIGHT!!

(He pours Potion One into Potion Two. He waits.) And we wait. *(He waits.)*

And we . . . continue waiting. *(He continues waiting, nothing happens.)*

Tomorrow, it happens, Pedro. TOMORROW!

An Imagination Question for the Actor

What was the SUPERFORMULA?

EDDIE THE NINJA

Eddie is a very intense but not-so-good martial arts instructor.

It is not like getting a library card, young man. You must learn that first. Being a ninja is very VERY serious stuff. NINJA stuff . . . They give you ninja stars, and you get to learn swords and—most importantly—you get to learn the mind techniques of the ninja.

And these techniques you must use only for the powers of good . . . or at least for the powers of looking REALLY cool at parties.

I am ninja.

My eyes are sharp like tiger's teeth. My hands are fast as lightning bolts on a winter morning. My mind is fast like a . . . like a really REALLY fast train.

An Imagination Question for the Actor

Who do you think Eddie is talking to?

EDGAR THE SLEEPY CAT

Edgar is a cat. For no particular reason, he's always sleepy. He rubs his eyes because he probably just woke up.

Hey . . . good morning. What time is it? Is it dinner yet? Last thing I remember was lunch. I had a steak enchilada and a slice of sausage pizza and some flan and some carrot cake—you need those carrots, gotta stay healthy.

Man, that sausage pizza was good. Paw-licking good, man. Is there any more? How about flan? Is there any more flan? Or did my fat owner eat it all? That's all he does, man. I'm telling you. He eats and sleeps and eats more. It's a miracle he gets anything done.

Hey, wake me up if you see him. I'm gonna take a little nap. Right here, actually. *(He lies down.)* When I wake up, there better be more carrot cake.

An Imagination Question for the Actor

Other than rubbing his eyes, how else might Edgar show us he's sleepy?

ENRIQUE THE COP

Enrique is a cop in a really boring town where nothing ever happens.

Being cop is like being in the world of action, in the call of duty, the line of fire, at all times. You gotta be in tip-top shape, and you gotta be ready, EVERY DAY, to save people from all kindsa stuff.

Just yesterday I helped this one lady—she didn't know which way the post office was. She was like, "Is it this way down Fifty-fourth?" I was like, "No, lady, it's not. It's actually down Fifty-sixth." She was like, "Oh, thank you, young man. Thank you, officer." And that was that.

Can you imagine that poor lady? Looking around on Fifty-fourth? "Where am I? I'm so lost! OH, NO?!" Woulda been CRAZY. Lucky I got to her.

I mean, I don't wanna make it sound like I'm patting myself on the back, but . . . we do a lot more than eat doughnuts, is all I'm saying. What is that? Are those Danishes? Yum.

An Imagination Question for the Actor

How long do you think Enrique has been a cop?

ERNESTO THE PERSONAL TRAINER

It seems Ernesto is full of energy. He's teaching a group of guys how to lift weights.

Hey, man. Come on, guys. Let's do this! Come on! This isn't just weight lifting! This is your life we're talking about! This isn't just personal training, this is your whole everything training! Let's DO IT!

(He lifts some weights.) One, two, one, two—COME ON! PUMP THAT IRON, BABY! FEEL THAT BURN! It's incredible! Feel that muscle tissue, man! Push those muscles until they hurt, dude. Anything else isn't even worth it, bro!

AAAGHHH!!! YEAH!!! One, two, three, four. One, two, three, four. COME ON! I've been doing this all day and look at me! I'm in great shape! COME ON! PUSH IT TO THE LIMIT!

One, two . . . *(He collapses. A beat. He pops right back up.)* Three, four. YEAH! GOOD JOB! WOO!

How long was I out?

An Imagination Question for the Actor

What do you imagine Ernesto is wearing?

FELIX THE LUMBERJACK

Felix wears flannel, maybe he even holds an axe—a fake one, kids. He's sweaty from a hard day's work.

One more coming down!!! *(He covers his ears. A tree falls.)*

I do this all day. I'm a lumberjack. My friends are always telling me, "Felix, how do you do it? How do you cut down trees all day, don't you feel bad?" First thing I tell them is: "How much do you like toothpicks?" They say: "WHAT?!"

I say: "Next time you're at a restaurant or something and you gotta piece of *bistec empanizado* or some *frijoles* stuck in your teeth, and you need to NOT look like an idiot, you think of me. 'Cause without lumberjacks there are no toothpicks." That normally shuts 'em right up.

ONE MORE COMING DOWN! MOVE OVER, GUYS!

An Imagination Question for the Actor

What's Felix's favorite smell?

FLACO THE ASTRONAUT

After years of working very hard, Flaco became an astronaut. Here, he's in a spaceship talking to his brother about what it's like to see the earth from space.

You haven't lived until you've seen the earth from space, Tomas. You have no idea. It's the most amazing feeling, bro. It's like suddenly all the training and all the hard work I had to put in and all the time at the air force and all the science classes and all the tests and the whole thing is suddenly worth it, just like that, totally WORTH IT.

You know what it's like? It's like this glass ball, bro. It's like this beautiful little glass ball floating through space. It's weird. I'm up here. You're there. And I can see it all.

All of the earth. And it's this special little place, Tomas. You gotta get up here.

An Imagination Question for the Actor

What do you imagine the earth looks like from space?

GABE THE PILOT

Gabe is an airplane pilot. He's also eight.

Attention, passengers. This is your pilot, Gabe, speaking.

We're gonna be reaching our cruising altitude of forty-thousand feet in about a minute. We anticipate a smooth ride on your flight from Miami to Chicago, today.

Now I know what a lot of you might be thinking. "Honey, how old do you think that pilot is?" Well, I want you to know, that even though I'm only eight, I'm licensed, I'm certified, and I passed art with an A-plus 'cause Mrs. Diaz thinks I'm the most talented kid in the whole grade. So sit back, relax, eat a little bag of pretzels, read a newspaper someone else left behind, and don't worry about a thing. Gabe, your pilot, is in control.

Oh my gosh, dude, what's that button do? . . . Just kidding.

A Hidden-Clue Question for the Actor

Where is Gabe flying?

GORDO THE NEWS ANCHOR

Gordo is a news anchor. He talks straight into a camera with a cheesy smile and a bad haircut.

Hello, big city. It's Gordo Hernandez, your favorite big-city news anchor. You're watching Channel Four.

Today, in the news: A shipment of cinnamon buns on its way to Milander Elementary School didn't quite make it, today. The Cinnamon Bun Company truck overturned on highway sixteen, and the back doors popped open, and over a thousand cinnamon buns were scattered all over two miles of highway. Witnesses and police officers called it quite the "sticky" situation.

(He stops talking to the camera, starts talking to someone in the studio with him.) Come on, guys. You see what I have to work with here? You see the garbage they feed me? These lines? How am I supposed to work with these lines? That was AWFUL. "Sticky" situation? Are you kidding? Who laughs at that? Monkeys? I'm going over to Channel Seven. You think I'm kidding?

An Imagination Question for the Actor

What would a thousand cinnamon buns scattered on the highway look like?

GUILLERMO THE TRAIN CONDUCTOR

Guillermo is a train conductor in a busy city on a busy day. He's very stressed out and has been screaming at passengers all day.

Next stop, Grand Heights! Stand clear of the closing doors! HEY, LADY! Are you on the train or are you off? COME ON! Make a decision! *MUJER! POR FAVOR!* Stand clear of the closing doors.

(He turns and speaks directly to us.) This job is harder than it looks, *hermano*. When I first came to this country, my brother told me this was a great way to make money. "No stress," he said. I don't think he ever rode the train at rush hour.

HEY, BUDDY, how many suitcases are you trying to fit on here?! AND YOU! LADY! Pick your kid off the floor. You know how dirty that is? What's this look like? Your mama's house?!

Stand clear of the closing doors!

An Imagination Question for the Actor

What does Guillermo's train smell like?

GUSTAVO THE MALL SECURITY GUARD

Gustavo is wearing what looks like a policeman's uniform, only he's not a policeman. He works at the mall.

First thing in the morning, I stop by the Food Court. I pick up some tacos, maybe some Bourbon chicken at the Chinese place.

I make my way around the back to the parking lot. Sometimes some kids try to get cute and skateboard all around that place. I kick 'em out if I find 'em. If I don't, I know all that means is I have to come back again later.

I go down to the department stores and say hi to the perfume ladies. They're all my friends. One of 'em thinks I'm cute. Or at least, I think she thinks I'm cute.

Lunchtime rolls back around I swing by the Food Court again. Grab a smoothie or something. I watch my diet.

In the afternoon, mostly, all I do is return lost kids to their parents, lost purses to their owners, that sort of thing. It's not fancy-schmancy, but I make a difference wherever I can, man.

An Imagination Question for the Actor

Does Gustavo like the mall?

HECTOR THE P.E. COACH

Coach Hector is strict. He teaches P.E., so he has a whistle and wears high socks and weird shorts.

Good morning. My name is Coach Hector. Now I know it's only the first day of the third grade for a couple of you, but I want to lay down some ground rules, first things first. OK? A couple rules for a successful day in physical education.

Rule One. No hitting. Rule Two. Water breaks are at the END of class only. I don't want any of you drinking up a gallon of water and getting all cramped up and crying on the floor of my gymnasium. Rule Three. No spitting. No laughing. No talking. No running unless I tell you to run. No walking if you're supposed to be running.

And no smiling unless I say it's OK to smile. Any questions?

A Hidden-Clue Question for the Actor

What happens when kids drink a gallon of water?

IVAN THE DENTIST

Ivan wears a dentist's lab coat. He also wears rubber gloves.

All I want to do is help kids, but what do I get in return? Crying faces, screaming kids. They all hate me. ALL OF THEM. They hate me.

Nobody likes a dentist.

I don't wanna hurt you! Trust me! I don't! I wanna make it all feel better! I wanna clean your molars and get rid of your cavities and teach you to floss! Just 'cause I'm a dentist doesn't mean I'm evil!

I should have been a vet. Everyone likes veterinarians. They help puppies and cats, and everyone thinks they're just the nicest people in the world.

Not me. I'm a monster. I'm the guy with the drill. I'm everyone's worst nightmare.

An Imagination Question for the Actor

Why do you think Ivan became a dentist?

JAVIER THE JANITOR

Javier is a janitor. He's tired of kids littering.

HEY, KIDS! You think it's cute to litter, but it's not. You think it's cute to leave your little juice boxes on the floor, but it's not. You think it's cute to play "Let's Throw the Leftovers from the Pizza Party at Each Other after School," but it's not.

These kids these days, *son unos asquerosos*, I swear. Back in my country no one littered, and if they did, we called them *cochinos*, and they felt stupid, and they picked it up.

You kids here. You got it easy. No one screams at you. Or, at least, if anyone is screaming at you, it isn't working. So I'm here. Javier the janitor is here to tell you it ain't cute.

An Imagination Question for the Actor

What does the word "cochino" mean?

JOHN THE SPORTS FAN

John wears a Mets T-shirt. He's cheering at a game. He talks to us every so often.

Vamos! Go Mets! You can do it, guys!

You see these guys? I love 'em. The Mets were my dad's team. Papi LOVED the Mets. Even when they lost, which was A LOT.

The Mets were Papi's team, and they were Abuelo's team, and so that's why, even when they're on a losing streak, like they are this year, I'm still here, in the stands, cheering like nobody's business. No matter what, I got my season tickets, and I got a hot dog, and I'm here, and I'm the first in line at every game. And I'm the last one to leave.

'Cause if I scream loud enough, it sounds almost like they're here with me.

GO METS! *VAMOS!* YEAAAH!

A Hidden-Clue Question for the Actor

What's John's favorite food at baseball games?

JORGE THE LIBRARIAN

Jorge is a librarian. He speaks in a very loud whisper. He wants some pesky kids to shut up. His English is not so great.

Oye! Shhh. This isn't a rock concert, young man. You can't just scream your little lungs out whenever you want, wherever you want, why-ever you want, *hijo*. This is a library.

Who am I? I'm Jorge. I'm the librarian. I've worked here for seventeen years. That means you're on MY turf, on MY territory, in MY house. You got that? And this is a place of learning, of reading, of education-ing.

This isn't some place for you and your friends to come in here screaming like this is some kind of wrestling match on the TV. So, shhh.

(He waits for them to get quiet. They do.)
That's better.

A Hidden-Clue Question for the Actor

How long has Jorge been a librarian?

JOSÉ THE PIZZA DELIVERY GUY

José is a pizza delivery guy. He just showed up at a customer's door with a big pizza order.

Hey. What's up? Sorry I'm late, the traffic was killer, bro. OK, so I got three large cheese pizzas and two medium sausage-and-olive pizzas. I got two bottles of diet soda and an order of garlic rolls.

(The customer complains.) You ordered two medium vegetable pizzas? Well what do you want me to do with these medium sausage-and-olive pizzas?

(The customer complains.) I dunno. Why don't you just take the sausages off?! Leave the olives on, that's like a vegetable, right?

(The customer complains.) No, no, no, man. Don't call my manager. I need this job. I don't like this job, but I need this job, dude. Fine. Look. I'll take all the sausage off myself, see?

(José starts taking the sausage off the pizza.) Oh, this is gross.

An Imagination Question for the Actor

What kind of car does José drive?

JULIAN THE FOOTBALL PLAYER

Julian is a professional football player. He's very aggressive when he speaks.

I've been playing professional football for years. A lot of people think my job is barbaric. That means I'm some kind of barbarian. Like all I do is run around all day and smash my head into things, but it's a lot more than that. Sometimes, I smash my head into people, too.

And most of the time, these people don't want to have me smash into them, or sometimes, if I'm lucky, they're holding a football, and my job isn't done until there's grass in their teeth and they dunno what to do with themselves.

When I was a little kid, my abuela always wanted me to play tennis.

I said to her, "*Nunca, Abuela.*" Then I smashed my head into her rocking chair.

An Imagination Question for the Actor

What other sports might Julian enjoy playing?

LAZARO THE FOOT DOCTOR

Lazaro stands with his hands far from his face. They smell.

There's nothing fancy about my job. I get to say, "Hey, I'm a doctor," but when people ask what KIND of doctor, well, that's when things get weird.

I'm a podiatrist. That means I deal with feet. Like on the end of your legs, like stinky cheese smell, like FEET. And that means, unfortunately for me, no matter how many rubber gloves I wear, no matter how many times I wash my hands . . .

(He smells his hands. They're gross.) Oh, man. And it's not like my patients are dirty. Some of them are really nice people. Mrs. Fernandez wears tons of perfume and expensive necklaces and everything, but you get close to her feet.

(He smells his hands.) And you won't forget it for weeks.

An Imagination Question for the Actor

Why did Lazaro become a podiatrist?

LUIS THE CHEF

Luis is a chef who loves his job. Here, he talks to customers about the delicious dinner he's about to make them.

Tonight? Tonight what I got for you is *una delicia.* It's *pura magia* in your mouth.

I'm gonna make you some *pollo asado* with a side of *fufu de platanos* and a delicious *flan de coco* for dessert.

Your mouth is gonna water for days after just thinking about how delicious my cooking is. Your mind is gonna wander when you're at work, and you should be working instead of thinking about how delicious my dinner was.

Get ready. *Aqui viene. Buen provecho!*

Imagination Questions for the Actor

What are each of the foods Luis describes? Have you ever eaten any of them?

MANNY THE TRUCK DRIVER

Manny is a well-read and very smart truck driver. He drives while he talks.

"The road to the City of Emeralds is paved with yellow brick." That's the Wizard of Oz.

I'm a truck driver. I spend a lot of time on the road. Driving. Not yellow brick ones, but you get my drift. Drift. Hah.

"The words of my book nothing, the drift of it everything." That's Whitman. He's a writer. I spend a lot of time on the road. And mostly, what I spend my time doing, is listening to books on tape. I learn a lot that way.

"Uneasy lies the head that wears the crown." That's Shakespeare. But you know what I say? "Uneasy lies the head that doesn't have a good audiobook." That's me. I wrote that. I stink. But, hey . . . That's why I drive trucks.

An Imagination Question for the Actor

What books would you listen to on a long road trip?

MARCELO THE LIFEGUARD

Marcelo is a lifeguard. He has a whistle. He wears a bathing suit and sunblock.

(He yells at someone in the water.) Hey, little kid! Get back to the shore! You're way too close to the rip current! You gotta come back! Good!

(He turns and looks at us.) Being a lifeguard is pretty much the coolest job in the whole world. I just gotta make sure no one drowns or anything, which is a piece of cake. Other than that? I get to sit on the beach and watch the water. I got like the most perfect tan you've ever seen. And once in a while a whale beaches itself, and I'm on the six o'clock news.

(He yells at a kid again.) Hey buddy, come on! Get back in here! Come on! You're too far out! You're TOO FAR OUT!

(He looks at us really quick.) This always works. *(He yells one last thing at the kid.)* SHARK! *(He looks back at us, proud, as the kid comes back.)* Told you.

Imagination Questions for the Actor

Have you ever been to a beach? If you have, what was it like? If you haven't, what do you imagine it was like?

MARIO THE PIRATE

Mario is from Venezuela. He's also a pirate.

Being a pirate? Awesome. Being a Venezuelan pirate? A little weird.

You wouldn't know it, but all the other pirate guys are like, "Arrrrg mate-y!" at the weekly pirate meetings, and I'm all like, "*Hola chicos, como estan?*" and they look at me funny. They're all from England or wherever else, and they think I'm weird, and I don't belong, just 'cause I'm from Venezuela.

I dress like this just to fit in. The puffy shirt, the red belt. This isn't really my style, but you gotta make friends, right?

I mean, I keep asking, but I don't think they're gonna let me in the club permanently, which is OK, because I don't really like the food they serve at weekly pirate meetings anyway. Just one *arepa*! That's all I'm asking for!

An Imagination Question for the Actor

What's an arepa?

MIGUELITO THE CANDY MAKER

Miguelito is a candy maker. He has a long pointy moustache and talks very loudly because he's used to selling his products on loud street corners.

Hola! My name is Miguelito! My job is simple and wonderful all at the same time! I am a candy maker. I know, it sounds like a wonderful thing, but it's not all easy and fun. Candy making is hard work. I have to get up very early to make my delicious cavity-causing yum-yums. Take this candy for instance, it's called pirulin.

(He holds out a pirulin. It's small and shaped like a cone.) Pirulin is a little cone-shaped, delicious candy-on-a-stick that the kids like to eat day and night. It's hard getting the cute little stripes in there, making the colors perfect, all that.

You think this happens easy? This is not bubble gum. This isn't even *churros*, man. This is serious stuff. To you, maybe it's just some junk you buy for fifty cents, but to me, this is some hard work. *(He eats it.)* Some delicious hard work.

An Imagination Question for the Actor

What's your favorite candy?

MR. NELSON, THE MOST BORING TEACHER MAYBE EVER

Mr. Nelson is a very boring teacher. No one listens in his class, and someone just threw a paper airplane at his face.

Who threw that? I'm serious. Who threw that? I get no respect from any of you. You think it's funny to throw spitballs and paper airplanes at hard-working teachers? You think that's just adorable, don't you? Well, let me tell you something, kid, it's not.

You think it's easy being boring? I KNOW I'm boring. I know I am, but what am I supposed to do? You think this is fun for me? It's not. Not really. It USED to be fun, but not anymore. Now it's a paycheck. You understand? My teaching you, it's just about me paying the rent. OK?

I don't wanna be here any more than you do, kid. You understand that? I wanna be at home reading science journals as bad as you wanna be home playing PlayStation, but that's not gonna happen. I'm getting paid to do a job, and the government says you have to learn about social sciences. So get out your notebooks.

I SAID GET OUT YOUR NOTEBOOKS. It's gonna be a long day.

A Hidden-Clue Question for the Actor

What class does Mr. Nelson teach?

OMAR THE BARBER

Omar is a friendly neighborhood barber.

Oye, Pepito, get over here. Sit in my chair. Go ahead, little man. *Vamos a ver*, look at that hair, bro. You should have come to me last week, maybe earlier. It's growing over your ears, you look like that little dude from *Lord of the Rings*, bro. "FROOODO! FROODOO!" It's something like that, right?

Hah. Ha, ha, ha. Oh man, so how do you want it? Your haircut. How you want it? Fade? Flat-top? What can I do for you, bro?

An Imagination Question for the Actor

How do you like your hair cut?

OSCARITO THE SKATEBOARD KID

Oscar holds a skateboard in one hand. He talks with attitude. His knees are bandaged. He points to them.

That's from when I spilled out pretty bad over by Food Mart. I was gonna go up for a big finish, but I ended up landing on my knees instead. You don't get up good enough on the railing, BAM, this happens.

But this? This is nothing, man. You should see the stuff me and Fernie and Paulino do over at Gates Park, man. It's crazy. It's illegal, so you have to be real careful not to get caught by the cops, but it's pretty rad.

They call it "a waste of time" in school. It's not. It's a life. Some of our friends play video games, some of them read books.

To me? It's all a waste of time, bro. All of it.

An Imagination Question for the Actor

What hobbies do you love that someone might call a waste of time?

PEDRO THE MAILMAN

Pedro holds a satchel full of envelopes and packages.

Everyone loves Christmas. "Oh, Merry Christmas," everybody says, but not me, *hermano*.

In December, there's nothing I hate more than Christmas, *hermano*. It's not cute to have to carry around thousands of stupid Christmas cards, then the presents. Sometimes I have to work triple overtime just to get it done.

People should do less mailing of presents, less Internet shopping, man. Gimme a break, you know? Give my cute little white truck a break. That thing's delicate, you know? I mean, I DO kind of like seeing kids with their little faces in the windows when I'm coming around, but it's not THAT cute.

A Hidden-Clue Question for the Actor

What color is Pedro's truck?

PEPITO THE BIRD WATCHER

Pepito is a bit of a nerd. He has a pair of binoculars around his neck. He watches birds.

This your first time? It's not MY first time, that's for sure. I've been watching birds for a while. I started doing it with Abuelo. He taught me everything there is to know. Cardinals, blue jays, orioles, and those are just the baseball teams.

(He laughs at his own lame joke.) My favorite, though, and Abuelo's favorite, are the sparrows. People throw that word around a lot, just "sparrows," but there's really a whole world of species of them.

House sparrow, Spanish sparrow, cinnamon sparrow, plain-backed sparrow, Dead Sea sparrow, Cape sparrow, gray-headed, parrot-billed, Swahili, then there's the desert sparrow, the tree sparrow (you'll never guess where those live), and the Sudan golden sparrow.

You're not bored, are you? This is exciting. I think I see something. Are you asleep?

An Imagination Question for the Actor

Do you have a favorite animal?

THE PRINCIPAL

The principal is a chubby man with glasses. He talks very slowly.

Well . . . Oscar . . . You've been called to my office because . . . well . . . You know why you've been called to my office . . . Mrs. Martinez is very upset . . . at the prank you pulled . . . in her science class. There's nothing funny about . . . throwing Spanky . . . the class guinea pig . . . across the room . . . I don't care how good Victor is at catching . . . It's just not something that you do . . . Do you understand? Poor Spanky . . . is gonna have to go to the counselor's office for the next week. He won't stop shaking . . . poor fellow . . . You know . . . this isn't the first time it's happened to him . . . Last summer we had similar problems . . . Evan Gonzalez built a little catapult. It was very messy . . . You kids . . . where do you think this stuff up?

An Imagination Question for the Actor

How old is the principal?

RAMON THE PAINTBALL KING

Roberto is an annoying kid who is always trying to be funny.

This here is a semiautomatic BGD-13. It's top loaded, and the hopper holds over three hundred rounds of paintballs. The hard kind. The CO_2 tank in the back swaps out with a quick release pin, so just in case you're in the middle of the action when you're running out of air, all you gotta do is SHOOM-SHOOM-PING, and it's done, and you're ready to go.

I got a chrome double trigger that I put in with Papi and a built-in squeegee and a shoulder sling and an arm butt plate. Don't make jokes about the name of that.

I used to have a laser sight at the end of this thing, but that's too flashy. Too much. And too much is tacky.

It's a sport like any other, bro. Like soccer. But with guns that shoot paint.

An Imagination Question for the Actor

Is paintball anything like soccer?

RENIER, KARAOKE KING

Renier learned to speak English with a karaoke machine. He has a thick accent.

I don't know much English. But the English I know, I know from music.

My big brother had a karaoke machine. I used to sing with it all the time. It would show you the words to songs and you could sing them into a microphone.

When I came here from Uruguay, my mother said: "You have to learn English." I said to my mother, "Mami, I know English. Because I know Michael Jackson." She said, "WHAT?!"

And I explained to her. I said, "I know Michael Jackson. I know Bruce Springsteen. I know The Beatles. And Bone-Thugs-and-Harmony." My brother's machine? Karaoke? It was almost better than school.

I said ALMOST.

A Hidden-Clue Question for the Actor

Where did Renier come from?

RICKY THE MODEL-CAR MAKER

Ricky carefully puts a model car together. He talks to us, but hardly looks us in the eye. He's too focused.

"Insert part 14-A into 14-B." That's what it says in the instructions. You gotta follow the instructions, man, if not, the whole thing is basically garbage. And you gotta use the best glue. 'Cause if not, you can see the glue sticking stuff together, and that just looks bad.

This here? It's a 1991 Nissan 300Z. Special model. T-Top. See that? See the T-Top? I think I'm gonna paint the sides with slashes of water.

Not fire. Fire is dumb. Everybody does fire.
I'm gonna do water.

On the sides, real cool. Sick-nasty. And I'm also gonna— *(He tries to show us something, but his fingers are now stuck together.)* Oh, man. I use the best glue. Oh, man.

A Hidden-Clue Question for the Actor

What kind of car is he making?

ROBERTO THE FUTURE STAND-UP COMIC

Roberto is an annoying kid who is always trying to be funny.

Hey, what's WITH chocolate milk? They don't have this where I'm from, man. What is this? Is it dessert or is it a drink? Am I right? Huh? Jennifer? Benny? Anybody?

You don't see them mixing two things together at other parts of the lunch line. You don't see them giving you chicken-sandwich drink or chocolate meatloaf. All I'm saying is, it's one thing or it's another.

Am I right? Claudia? Anyone? Am I the only one who realizes this is crazy? And speaking of crazy, what's WITH juice boxes?

You ever tried to drink one of those things without a straw? Where's everyone going?

An Imagination Question for the Actor

What would you do to get Roberto to be quiet?

RODNEY THE AMATEUR MAGICIAN

Rodney is a magician, a very, VERY bad one. He holds a top hat in his left hand.

Hello, kids! How are you today? I am Rodney El Amazing, and I'm here, today, to do magic for you? Very good? Yes.

For my first trick, I will reach into this hat, and I will pull out a birthday cake for the birthday boy! He's turning four today! A four-year-old deserves a cake, right? How would you like that? Very good? Yes?

OK. Here we go. Get ready to see why Rodney El Amazing got the last name El Amazing. I put my hand in this hat. *(He does.)* I say the magic words: Doopity-Dee. Flippity Manyos. *Me gusta la torta, de cumpleaños*, and what do we have?!

(He pulls out a handful of messy, sloppy cake. He looks in his hat. It's all a mess now.) Can I get some paper towels?

A Hidden-Clue Question for the Actor

How old is the birthday boy?

RUBEN TABLE TENNIS CHAMPION

Ruben takes table tennis very seriously. He holds a little table tennis racquet. He's a prodigy.

I practice every morning. I swipe four hundred swings one way and four hundred swings the other way. Both hands. Each way. That makes about sixteen hundred target swings. That's one thousand six hundred.

That's a lot, but it's the only way. I've been playing since I was two. Gotta keep in shape. Table tennis isn't just some hobby: I'm a prodigy. They call me that. All the pros. The referees. All of them.

I'm Ruben the Prodigy. I'm Ruben the Marvel. I'm Ruben the Puerto Rican Table Tennis Phenomenon. *(He swipes.)* And don't you forget it.

A Hidden-Clue Question for the Actor

How long has Ruben been playing table tennis?

RUDY THE TOY COLLECTOR

Rudy is showing us his precious toy collection.

That over there is all my original Frankie Deluxe action figure stuff. That's my space landing war collection, and that over there—DON'T STEP ON THAT—is my Super Lightning Action Man play set.

My mom's been buying me this stuff for years. I told her, I said, "Mami, I don't want clothes. Don't get me socks. And I don't want books either. I want toys."

And she was like, "Your life can't all be playing and playing," and I said, "Mami, who said anything about playing?! This is collecting! I'm a collector, man."

Don't open those. They're still in the packaging for a reason.

An Imagination Question for the Actor

What do you collect?

SERGIO THE BIKE EXPERT

Sergio is wearing an intense bicycle helmet and bicycle gloves. He's probably also covered in mud.

You're gonna need back-pedal brakes, bro. For your BMX? Trust me. There ain't nothing like being at the top of a drop on a hill or on a mud slide or on a WHATEVER and getting your hand brake stuck. You want the back pedal. You want the control in your feet, not your hands. Your feet don't get tired like your hands do, and the last thing you want is your hands to be like giving out when they shouldn't be. Back pedal is the way to go, unless you wanna be coasting down a hill at like sixty miles an hour screaming your lungs out for your mami, getting slapped in the face with tree branches, sliding out, and flying forty feet in front of your bike, hitting rocks with your butt all the way down.

I didn't think so. Oh, and one more thing: you're gonna need a helmet.

A Hidden-Clue Question for the Actor

What kind of bike is Sergio talking about?

STEVIE THE DAREDEVIL

Stevie holds his dad's video camera. He talks to it. He's standing on top of the swings.

This is Stevie Gonzalez reporting. Recording on Papi's video camera. If someone finds this, and I'm nowhere to be found, it's because it worked. I'm about to jump off the swings at Milander Park. My favorite park. I'm about to maybe—possibly—fly away to Spain or to China like I've always wanted. I've done some research. I've done some reading. And plus I looked at tons of pictures in *Scientific Magazine* and *Flying Weekly* . . . but now? No more reading. No more waiting. Now this is time to get outside. Now this is time to get stuff done.

Do not try this at home, people. I'm six feet up in the air. My legs are dangling off of the end of this thing. And I'm about to let go. Ready?

(A pause. He's scared.) Ready? No more waiting. *(Another pause. He's really scared.)* Oh, man. *(He doesn't go anywhere.)* Oh . . . man.

A Hidden-Clue Question for the Actor

What's the name of Stevie's favorite park?

THE SUPERHERO

The superhero wears tights and a cape.
He stands very proud and speaks with a loud, booming voice.

I was born on a distant planet. This distant planet is a place where people can fly, and everyone has laser vision, and we can see in the dark and shoot electricity from our fingernails. So, when I came here, it was kinda obvious what I had to do. I had to save every innocent person on your planet and protect you from powerful evildoers.

So I did what any normal person would do: I bought some colorful tights and got a cape, got a special cave where I can hide and do all my research, and I got a snazzy car—even though I don't need one 'cause I can fly.

So don't fear, people. I'm here: Superheroman.

Don't worry about it. I'm working on a new name.

An Imagination Question for the Actor

What other special powers do you imagine this Superheroman might have?

TITO THE GADGET KID

Tito holds a remote control. He's a genius.

You see this? I built it. It looks like a remote control, yes, sure, but I programmed it so I can do the TV, the VCR, the DVD player, the air conditioner, the vacuum cleaner, and even Papi's car.

I'm good with electronics. And engineering. Some people like drawing. Some people like music.
For me? I see everything in sprockets and springs, circuits and indicator lights. When I was two years old, I took apart Tio Fernando's cell phone and put it back together without him ever even noticing.

Well, the screen turned blue and he kept getting weird calls from Japan, but—I mean, come on—
I was TWO.

An Imagination Question for the Actor

What were you like when you were two years old?

WILFREDO, MAMI'S FAVORITE

Wilfredo is dressed very nicely. His shirt is ironed. His hands are very clean.

My sisters don't like me. I have two, and neither of them do. They tell me all the time, just like that, they say, "Wilfredo, we don't like you," and I know why: I'm Mami's favorite.

She doesn't say it, no, she's never said it, but you can tell. Mami irons my shirts every morning, even my T-shirts. At dinner, she always serves me first, and she always serves me the most. She says, "For my *machito*." That means, "For my little macho man." I looked it up in the Spanish-English dictionary next to the desk near the kitchen.

And that's what I am. For sure. *(He makes sure his shirt looks good.)*

Her little *machito*.

A Hidden-Clue Question for the Actor

How many sisters does Wilfredo have?

50 Monologues for Girls

ABUELA

Abuela wears a housedress. Maybe she has curlers in her hair. She opens the fridge and gets really REALLY upset.

Who ate the *arroz con leche*?! I was saving that for Manolito. It's his favorite, and he only comes over the house twice a week, and last week the *arroz con leche* was a little watery, but I told him, I promised him not to worry because I'd make it again this week.

And I took half of the batch to church on Wednesday night, and Lupe and Francisco told me it was really very good, and the other half I put here. The other half was here, *AQUI*, in a plastic container in the Frigidaire next to the mustard and across from the cranberry juice—it's good for my kidneys—and someone—SOMETHING—ate Manolito's *arroz con leche.*

Who was it? WHO WAS IT?!

A Hidden-Clue Question for the Actor

What juice does Abuela think is good for the kidneys?

AMALIA THE ASTRONOMER

Amalia is a regular kid who happens to be obsessed with the stars.

The Dippers come in sizes: big and little. Over there's Orion's belt, that's the scorpion thing, and that over there, that's the Swan Eating the Turtle.

Abuelo taught me about the stars. The kids at school, they all say things like, "Oh, Amalia's a crazy freak, she's into stars," but it's not true. Just 'cause I don't like video games or ballet class or skateboarding that doesn't make me a freak. All it makes me is . . . is . . . is interested in stars.

Abuelo used to tell me all about the constellations. He used to make some up, too. Like the Swan Eating the Turtle one. I know that's fake. I'm not dumb. But I think it's a good name either way.

A Hidden-Clue Question for the Actor

Where is Orion's belt?

ANITA THE SALSA INSTRUCTOR

Anita wears a very tropical outfit—VERY tropical—with mangoes or flamingoes on her shirt. Something ridiculous. She's also got a lot of energy.

OK, *mujeres*. Like this: *(She demonstrates some awesome salsa moves.)*

One, one. Cha, cha, cha.
Two, two. Cha, cha, cha.
Like, that. Cha, cha, cha.
Good, yes. Cha, cha, cha.
Oh, kay. Cha, cha, cha . . .

Lourdes . . . LOURDES, you're stepping all over your own toes, you're a mess, *mijita*. Look at you. No one graduates from Anita's Salsa Academy dancing the way you do. I won't let you. Next thing you know you're at a wedding or something, and someone says a joke like, "Oh my gosh, Lourdes, where did you learn to dance?," and you say, "Anita's Salsa Academy," and then I go out of business. I cannot have that. Let's try again.

One, one. Cha, cha, cha.
Still, bad. Cha, cha, cha.

An Imagination Question for the Actor

Have you ever taken a dance class? What was it like?

BEATRIZ THE SHOE STORE LADY

Beatriz has huge hair. She's older, like in her fifties. She's what you call "larger than life," and she's very, very loud. She owns a shoe store. An old customer just walked in.

Ay, pero que linda. Look at her, she's all grown up.

I bet you don't even remember me, *mijita.* I bet you don't even remember Beatriz the shoe store lady. You don't, do you? You used to come into my shoe store when you were little like this— *(Beatriz indicates how little the girl used to be.)*

And you used to NEVER NEVER NEVER stay still when we tried to put little shoes on your feet, you used to be like "NOOOOOO," and we'd have to hold you down just to get your little boots on.

Let me see those feet! Oh, come on, please, let me see how much we've grown up. *(Beatriz looks at the girl's feet.)* Well. Well. Let's see . . . *mijita.* What size are you these days? I'll see what I have in the back.

An Imagination Question for the Actor

How long do you think Beatriz has owned the shoe store?

BELA THE EVIL BABYSITTER

Bela has crazy eyes. Her hair is a mess. She's an evil babysitter.

Little children! Little children come downstairs! YOU. YOU. What is your name? Mario? What kind of name is Mario? Who are you, a video game?

Sit down. Sit down and listen good. Your parents left me with very strict instructions—young lady, sit down. They said that I have to make sure you're in bed by eight o' clock. YOUNG LADY, I SAID SIT DOWN. YES, YOU. Yes, next to Luigi . . . Mario, whatever his name is.

This is my first job babysitting for your parents, and so I want to make a good impression. I heard they tip very well, and I want to make sure they ask me back, is that OK? Good babysitting jobs don't come too often in this part of the city, and I don't want to mess this up.

So it's seven o'clock now. I say let's go ahead a little early. I say let's get ready for bed—DON'T YOU DARE INTERRUPT ME, YOSHI—whatever your name is.

An Imagination Question for the Actor

How does Bela dress?

CAROLINA THE SOCCER STAR

Carolina wears cleats, shin guards, the works. She holds a soccer ball.

My father was Antonio Fernandez-Fernandez. He was a soccer player in Argentina. He was amazing. He went to the World Cup three times . . . not as a player, but he went.

I've been playing soccer since before I could even walk. *(She does a trick with the ball.)* I never got rattles or fluffy stuffed animals, I got this. *(She kicks the ball.)* I don't mind, though. It's pretty cool being on the soccer team at school.

I'm a midfielder. Most of the other girls are into cheerleading or chorus, but not me. That stuff's always been a little . . . I dunno . . . "prissy" for me.

Give me this. Give me cleats and a ball and an open field. Give me green grass stains on my shorts and a sweaty jersey. Give me the pulse-pounding excitement of scoring a goal with three seconds left in the game in the playoffs. Those girls can keep cheerleading all they want.

A Hidden-Clue Question for the Actor

What is a midfielder?

CELIA IS MISS WHINY

Celia whines and complains about everything. She's a pain to be around.

But I don't wanna go to church. Everything there is so boring. The people who sing there sing badly, and off key, and it hurts my ears, and the water fountain water tastes like public pools, and the priest is always like "amen, amen, amen," and I can hardly hear what he's saying, and Maria and Hernando are gonna be there, and I don't wanna see them 'cause Hernando is having a birthday party for his tenth birthday, and I want to be able to say that I'm sick 'cause I don't feel like going to Hernando's party 'cause his mom makes awful cakes, and she makes us play these dumb games, and his dad makes you wait like forever 'cause he always has to take pictures of everything, and anyway, I don't even like Hernando 'cause he smells like cats 'cause he has cats 'cause his mom won't let him get a dog 'cause she's weird or something.

I just don't wanna. I don't. I dooooon't. Pleeeease.

A Hidden-Clue Question for the Actor

How old is Hernando?

CLAUDIA THE FANCY PERFUME LADY

Claudia is a woman at a department store counter who sells fancy perfumes.

This here, this is Passion-Passion. It's our new scent from the Elegant Elegance Collection. It's got a hint of gardenia and a hint of raspberry blush. It's really something fantastic, but some people are allergic to it. Actually—most people are allergic to it. I have to tell you that, legally. Don't sneeze on the glass, please.

If you don't like that, we have some others in the Elegant Elegance Collection that are just *divino*.

We have Coconut Sunset, Happiness, Birds on a Wire, and—my other favorite—Twilight on Sunday Morning with Lemons.

I recommend Coconut Sunset. No one's allergic to it, except dogs. And cats. And most children.

An Imagination Question for the Actor

What is Claudia wearing?

MISS CLEAN

Miss Clean is a very weird girl obsessed with cleaning things and cleaning products. Here she shows us her cleaning closet.

This is where I keep the disinfectant. This is where I keep the brushes. And this . . . This is where I keep my favorite. This is where I keep the Pine-Sol. I normally have three to ten bottles at a time. You never know when you're gonna need to go Pine-Sol the whole house.

You can't use it on the kitchen table because the kitchen table is called a "porous" surface, and I had to learn that the hard way. I had to learn that the hard way when my dad made me memorize the back of the label and especially the part about "Pine-Sol is antibacterial on nonporous surfaces. It is not recommended for direct use on wood surfaces such as untreated hardwood floors and untreated kitchen tables."

But all in all, it's pretty much my favorite smell in the whole world. Just delicious. If I could wear this as a perfume, I would. You don't think I'm weird, do you?

A Hidden-Clue Question for the Actor

What does "porous" mean?

CONCHITA THE ANNOYING FUNDRAISER GIRL

(In one quick breath, without waiting for a response, she starts.) Hi, how are you, how's everything this fine evening, I'm fine, thank you.

I hate to bother you at dinnertime but I wanted to let you know about the exciting opportunity my school, Three Palm Elementary, is doing.

It's a fundraiser, and I'm selling seven kinds of chocolates in order to raise money for the Three Palm Elementary Space Day Excursion.

With your help and your purchase of ten chocolate bars or more, you could help the Three Palm Elementary Space Day Excursion become a reality. Not a dream from the past, but a reality of . . . of . . . today.

The Giggleworth Chocolate Company has taken a bunch of different chocolates from their inventory, stuff that might not have been best sellers but is still delicious, and donated them to the Three Palm Elementary fundraiser at no cost, so everything we collect goes straight to the Three Palm Elementary Space Day Excursion.

I have macadamia-cheesecake ketchup, I have hot mustard chocolate, and I have sugar-free mashed potato chocolate.

How many can I sign you up for?

An Imagination Question for the Actor

Can you think up some other bad chocolate bar flavors?

CRISTINA THE PRETTY PRETTY PRINCESS

Christina is dressed in pink, much like a fairy tale princess.

I'm in pink 'cause I'm a princess. Don't laugh. This is the official color of princesses. They decided it at a meeting a million years ago. All the kings and knights and servants went into a room and decided

that pink, the softest most adorable color of them all, should be just for princesses.

(A beat.) Fine. I'm not really a princess. My dad's not a king, he's an accountant. Mami's not a queen, she's a teacher. But that doesn't mean I'm not royalty. If not today . . . someday. Someday very soon.

Until then, I'm waiting. *(Another beat.)* Just waiting . . . here . . . in pink.

A Hidden-Clue Question for the Actor

What does Cristina's mother do for a living?

DANIELA THE TALKING COQUI FROG

Daniela is a Puerto Rican coqui frog.

COQUIIIII! Please don't laugh. I can't control it. It's like the hiccups. It's not funny, everyone I know makes fun of me—

COQUIIIII!— I'm a frog, you see. A Puerto Rican coqui frog, and all my friends, the birds, the antelope, even the cougar, they all make fun of me 'cause I have this thing. I just scream once in a while, and it's not like I scream something cool like "Save the rainforest" or "Merry Christmas," I just scream—

COQUIIIII! And I have to live with it. It's not as bad now. Imagine living in a house with thirteen brothers and sisters. It was like a—COQUIIIII!—party nonstop. All day. Every day. COQUIIIII!

Please don't laugh. I told you, it's like hiccups. It's practically a medical condition.

A Hidden-Clue Question for the Actor

Where is the coqui frog originally from?

DIANA THE NOT-SO-EVIL WITCH

Diana is dressed like a witch. Maybe she's green, maybe she has a wart, but she's not evil.

We have a bad reputation, my kind. Everyone thinks we're green. We're not. I had one aunt who was kind of green, but that's because she ate a lot of broccoli.

We don't fly around on brooms. I mean, I WISH I did—think about all the money I'd save on gas, it's better than a hybrid car—but we don't. We can't. Brooms? Brooms barely last like a month at your house. After using them, they get all warped out like a toothbrush. Can you imagine trusting one to fly you around? No, thank you.

I'm allergic to cats. I don't like boiling my stews. I use the microwave every chance I get. And most importantly, I'm not evil. That's a stereotype. I mean, once in a while I return a movie late at the video store, but that's about it. We're not all evil, witches. Well, that said, we're also not all very good singers, either. I can barely sing "Happy Birthday." So don't ask me to sing, 'cause I'm not good at all. I don't care what the musicals tell you.

A Hidden-Clue Question for the Actor

What does "stereotype" mean?

CATALINA THE WORST-EVER BALLERINA

Catalina wears an ill-fitting pair of tights and ballet slippers.

I'm awful at this. Like truly, deeply awful. I asked my mom to get me ballet classes this year instead of softball, and it was maybe the worst decision I could have ever made.

No one makes fun of me. They're all very nice. And my teacher is really nice too. I just . . . I just don't like it one bit. This thing fits weird. It's tight around my butt. That's weird.

We run around all day jumping and prancing. "Prancing." That's a good word for it. There's no winning in ballet. There's no points. There's no home runs. I mean—there's competition—but not really for me. I'm awful. I'm worse than awful. And my teacher says, "Everyone has to start somewhere," but I can't believe that. Not the way I move. I'm goin' back to softball.

A Hidden-Clue Question for the Actor

What sport did Catalina play before she started ballet lessons?

ELENA THE SUBWAY CONDUCTOR

Elena speaks very loudly. She wears a subway conductor's uniform and eats a ham sandwich.

When I was a kid growing up, my second-grade teacher—Mrs. Turner—used to ask everyone what it is they wanted to do when they grew up, and everyone always had the same lame answers. "Fireman, policeman, ballerina, lawyer," and if they were REALLY trying to get a good grade, they'd say "teacher."

(She leans into a microphone really quickly.) Stand clear of the closing doors. *(Then she talks to us again.)* Everyone laughed when I said, "subway conductor." They all thought I was kidding, but I wasn't. Not one bit. It's weird, but I just knew. From an early age. From the first time I remember ever riding the subway, I remember thinking, "I want that."

(She leans into a microphone really quickly.)
Next stop, city hall. Stand clear of the closing doors. *(Then she talks to us again, with attitude.)*
Something funny to you?

A Hidden-Clue Question for the Actor

What was Elena's second-grade teacher's name?

ELIANA THE CUBAN BAKERY LADY

Elena wears an apron. She works in a loud Cuban bakery.

YOU WANT *PASTELES*?! WHO WANTS *PASTELES*?! WHO'S NEXT IN LINE? YOU? YOU?! WHO? I'm sorry, I don't hear nothing too good. You have to scream into my good ear. YOU WANT *PASTELES*?!

(She leans in, trying to hear an order with her good ear.) You want what? Croissant? Ha, ha, ha. No, sorry. We don't make that, because that's from France, and this is a Cuban bakery, not a France bakery.

Don't try to make me feel stupid, *mijito*, we make a lot of things, but we don't make croissant, OK? You look in glass, you tell me what you want. There's *pasteles de carne, guayaba, guayaba y queso*, there's magdalenas, marielinas, and mayalinas . . .

What's a magdalena? It's like a croissant, but not really. It's different. And it's not French.

A Hidden-Clue Question for the Actor

What is guayaba?

SUPER EVA

Super Eva is dressed like a regular kid, only she has a towel draped over her back like a cape. She stands with her arms at her hips, like a proud superhero.

It's EXACTLY like in the comic books. I lead two lives. In one I'm totally normal, and I eat breakfast and fail math tests once in a while, and I have to do my bed or my mom grounds me.

And in the other . . . in the other life, I dash and I fly and I stop trains from crashing and my cape flaps softly in the wind. I have a sidekick named Roberto, and he and I save the city every day—EVERY DAY—from criminal masterminds like Dr. Bizarro and Evil Alligatorman and the notorious Mrs. Cravinski.

She's an evil mastermind, but she's also my math teacher. And I know there's something about her that's shady. I just . . . know it.

A Hidden-Clue Question for the Actor

What's Super Eva's sidekick's name?

ISABEL THE EVIL CHONGA BIG SISTER

Isabel is an evil chonga *big sister.*

Listen, Lissette. All I'm saying is: don't use my hair dryer no more. That's it. It ain't even a big deal. You're the one making it a big deal. I know we gotta share a bathroom, but I don't gotta share my . . . my . . . hair appliances or whatever with you. Your hair's nappy, you're gonna ruin it.

I know the hairdryer don't never touch your hair, but you're still gonna ruin it! And anyway you break everything you touch 'cause you got *mano mala*. That's what Tia Paola calls it: *mano mala*. It's a superstition. It's a whatever.

I dunno what it means, it means "bad hands" or "evil hands" or "everything-you-touch-you-break hands," it means SOMETHING, and she's right. So don't ever touch my hair dryer ever again. Or my brushes. Or my toothbrush. Or the sink.

An Imagination Question for the Actor

Do any of your family members believe in superstitions?

KATY THE CAFETERIA LADY

Katy speaks very broken English. She's a sweet, older cafeteria lady.

Next! *Que quieres, mijita*? Meatloaf? Meatloaf?! No, today, we no have meatloaf. Today we have chicken sandwich, today we have mash potato, today we have green beans.

No. No pizza. We no have pizza today. Pizza we have Thursday. Today we have chicken sandwich. Mash potato. Green bean. OK. You want mash potato? OK. You want green beans?

You need you beans. YOU NEED YOU GREEN BEANS! Good for you, making you strong, making you good. Better for you than meatloaf.

You no want meatloaf. Believe me, *mijita*. I make meatloaf. I see what I put in meatloaf. You no want meatloaf.

An Imagination Question for the Actor

Do you have a favorite cafeteria worker? What's his or her name?

LAURA THE SCHOOL-CROSSING GUARD

Laura wears an orange vest. She has a whistle. She's about your mom's age. She helps kids cross the street because it's her job.

Red light gone. OK. Come on now. Green means walk. Walkin', walkin', walkin'. Let's go, kids. Come on, get to class. Get to school. Gotta learn stuff. Open those books. Do that classwork. No paper airplanes. Come on. Yellow. Get off, get—

(She blows the whistle.) I said, YELLOW, GET ON THAT SIDEWALK! *(She blows the whistle.)* Thank you. Red light. Stop. Wait. Stop. Wait. Wait . . . Wait. Almost, almost—

(She blows the whistle.) GET YOUR FEET OFF THE STREET! Thank you very much. You wanna get squashed like a cockroach under somebody's Hummer? Huh? I didn't think so.

(The light changes. The kids can walk.) Red light gone. OK. Come on now. Green means walk. Walkin', walkin', walkin'.

An Imagination Question for the Actor

What other jobs require whistles? Why?

LESLIE, MY FRIEND'S ANNOYING MOM

Leslie is your friend's annoying mother who wears too much lipstick and drives a sports car when she should be driving a minivan.

Oh, well look at you. Don't you look . . . *(She can't find the word, so she settles on:)* special. Ready for the big night? You and Margie going to the big spring dance? You all excited? Three boys asked Margie to the dance. How many boys asked you?

None? That's OK, sweety. Someday. Don't you worry about it. Someday. You should do something about your hair next time. You should do something more . . . I dunno. You should wash it, at least.

You did wash it? Well. Coulda fooled me. What kind of conditioner does your mom have you using? I know you're only nine, but it's never too early to start worrying about conditioner. If you conditioned your hair, maybe three boys would've asked you to the big dance. Like Margie.

Did I tell you three boys asked her? Three. That's more than none, sweety, that's all I'm saying.

A Hidden-Clue Question for the Actor

What dance is Margie going to?

LILIANA THE ADVENTURER

Liliana stuffs a backpack for what seems like a very exciting trip.

You got extra batteries? For your flashlight? You're gonna need 'em. You might wanna pack some more bandages. You never know out there. It gets crazy. Your knees get scraped up—last thing you want is to be bleeding on your socks.

Bottle of water? Map? Compass? It gets crazy. Sunscreen? I know it's nine o'clock at night, but you never know. One minute, you're out there just adventuring, having a good time, next thing you know, you've been out there for three days and you're collecting rainwater in your shoes and you're fighting an alligator with your bare hands. Haven't you ever seen *The Adventurer* on Discovery Channel?

I know it's just my backyard, but it's a big backyard. Kinda big. It's not small.

Fine. Make fun of me. It's not gonna be so funny when you wake up in quicksand.

A Hidden-Clue Question for the Actor

Where does Liliana imagine she's going to be collecting rainwater?

LOURDES ON THE BARNYARD FIELD TRIP

Lourdes is a prissy student on a field trip to a barnyard. Everything around her grosses her out.

This is gross. This is disgusting. I'm never eating meat again. I'm never even drinking milk again. Is that a goat? What is that? This is the worst field trip ever. A barnyard? A BARNYARD? This is crazy. What happened to museums and art galleries and Sea World. What kinda field trip is this? Everything here smells like public bathroom and mulch.

That thing's drooling. What is that? Is that a donkey or something? This isn't cute. This is just gross and weird, and the tour guide hardly has any teeth. I thought field trips had to be educational.

This is not educational. This is gross-u-cational. I wanna go to Sea World.

An Imagination Question for the Actor

What was your least favorite field trip?

LUZ THE CAMP COUNSELOR

Luz is a perky camp counselor who loves her job a little too much.

This is my seventh summer spent at St. Lucia's Day Camp, and I can't tell you how much fun you're going to have! My name is Luz, and that means "light," and I hope to be the light that lights up your days here at St. Lucia!

During the days, we have swimming and crafts, then at night we have super-scary-spooky stories around the campfire with Travis. Travis is a great storyteller —and he's kinda funny and has a six-pack and drives a Jeep, so that makes him supercute.

If it's your first summer here, I can't tell you how jealous I am. I remember my first summer at St. Lucia. It was like my whole life started all over again, like someone pressed the reset button on the Nintendo of my life. You're all gonna have SO much fun.

Who wants to make cookies?

A Hidden-Clue Question for the Actor

Who tells stories around the campfire?

MALENA THE CHUPACABRA HUNTER

Malena wears leather gloves and goggles. She might even be wearing body armor of some kind. She has a slingshot in her back pocket. She's determined.

It's a monster of mythical origin and legendary proportions. It's been terrorizing the country where my father was born for many years. It attacks whenever it wants and whatever it wants. It has fangs and devil eyes, and it'll suck your brains out of your head if it feels like it. It's called the Chupacabra. And I'm going to hunt it down.

Now I know what many of you may be thinking: Malena, you're not even old enough to drive. But I'll kindly remind you of the story in the Bible about David and Goliath. David could hardly drive. And Goliath was like a huge crazy monsterman. And I think we all know what happened when David decided to hunt down Goliath because he had killed all the *cabras* in Puerto Rico.

I got my slingshot ready. Let's do this.

A Hidden-Clue Question for the Actor

Where is the Chupacabra from?

MARIBEL THE SCHOOL POLICE OFFICER

Maribel is a school police officer. She takes her job VERY seriously and is VERY suspicious of every kid at her elementary school.

Excuse me, young man. What's that in your pocket? Young man. EXCUSE ME, YOUNG MAN. WHAT'S THAT IN YOUR POCKET?!

Do I need to search you? Do I need to— *(She talks into a walkie-talkie.)* I'm gonna need backup. This is Officer 3-13 requesting backup.

(She talks back to the kid.) Oh, you asked for it now. Get against the wall, Junior. What do I look like to you, your mama?! What's in your pocket? Do you have a weapon? What is that, is that some kind of—

(She pulls something out of his pocket. A pause. She's embarrassed. She gets back on the walkie-talkie.) Hey, this is Officer 3-13. That was a . . . that was a false alarm. Over . . . Yeah. It was . . . the kid had a glue stick. I repeat. It was a suspicious glue stick, that's all.

(Back to the kid.) Move along, buddy. Move along, kids, nothing to see here.

A Hidden-Clue Question for the Actor

What was in the kid's pocket?

MRS. MARTA THE ART TEACHER

Mrs. Marta teaches an art class. Octavio, a kind of a rebel, insists on doing his own thing.

Get out your brushes. Get your paints. You're gonna need green and brown. Today we're going to paint a forest. Paint a forest, very nice. Give the trees trunks. Nice. You're gonna need blue. Paint a lake. A nice, beautiful lake in the middle. Good. Get your yellow. A forest is nothing without the sun. Good. Great. Nice. Now you have to . . .

(She stops at Octavio's desk. He never follows instructions.) Octavio, what is this? *(Octavio doesn't answer.)*

Octavio is that a ninja robot? Octavio what did I tell you about painting ninja robots? Today's assignment was not to paint ninja robots. Today's assignment was to paint a forest, a BEAUTIFUL forest with green leaves and blue lakes and tree trunks. You ALWAYS do this. Why can't you just paint tree trunks?

(Octavio nervously paints something on his paper.) Good. Now your ninja robot has a forest. See? Isn't that better? Isn't it? Actually . . . actually . . . it looks kind of cool, doesn't it?

(She talks to the class.) Everyone, pull out some black paint. And red for the ninja sword. Right? We're all adding ninja robots.

A Hidden-Clue Question for the Actor

What color did Octavio paint the sword?

MAYLIN THE MAKEUP ARTIST

Maylin has a kit full of makeup supplies. She does makeup for a famous actress.

Ay. You need more blush. Lean in. Here. Lean in again. Good. You got eye boogers. Here's a cotton swab. Use it. Jeesh, did you even shower this morning? You're not making this easy on me, that's for sure. None of you do. Pucker up. Lipstick time.

Ay, don't complain, you know you love it. What color, this one or this one? This one's better for your eyes, this one'll make your lips pop more. Good. There. Good. Your hair looks like you got in a fight with a pitbull. What products are you using? I do makeup, not hair, but I can tell you that's a bad idea. Especially with your complexion. Open that eye. Good. Close it. Open the next. Good.

(She holds a mirror.) You look about thirty times better than when you walked in here. You're lucky to have me around.

An Imagination Question for the Actor

What famous actress would you like to do makeup for?

MERCY THE WILD ANIMAL EXPERT

Mercy talks straight into a camera. She's a wildlife expert filming a television show.

Now here in the backyard what we have is a black-haired Tasmanian Devil. The Tasmanian Devil—in my field, called *Sarcophilus harrisii*—is a carnivore. That means he eats *carne*, and that's meat. He's a marsupial like the kangaroo, and he's found in the wild only in Australia, in a crazy island place called Tasmania.

It looks a whole lot like a dog, but it's not. It's actually the largest carnivorous marsupial in the world. Look at those teeth! Like a skunk, it produces a crazy bad smell when it's scared and screeches the loudest most vicious noises you could ever imagine. It's a— *(She notices something, suddenly terrified.)*

Wilson! It's looking right at me. *(She notices something else.)* There's two of them. Three. No . . . six. There's six of them. Pack the camera. PACK THE CAMERA!

You hear that screech?! MOVE, WILSON, MOVE! The *Sarcophilus harrisii* are coming!

A Hidden-Clue Question for the Actor

Where would one find a Tasmanian devil?

MICAELA THE LIFEGUARD

Micaela is a lifeguard.

Hey! Come back from there! You can't be out that far! Come on, lady! Get your skinny kids out of the rip current! Come on! *(She dabs sunscreen on her face.)* Being a lifeguard looks like hard work, but trust me, it's not. Wait a second. That was backwards. I meant it the other way around. Being a lifeguard looks like easy work, but trust me, it's not.

You know how much water I drink every day? Six gallons. And I don't take bathroom breaks 'cause I don't need to. I sweat it out, every ounce, and sometimes I even get home thirsty. The pay is decent. Sunscreen is included. That's a plus. And, of course, there's the cute surfer boys. *(She strikes a pose.)* They love me.

OH! And once in a while, I get to save a life. I get to run out there and blow my whistle and pull some poor person outta the water and give 'em CPR and everyone cheers. I love that. I love when they cheer.

YO! LADY! WHAT DID I TELL YOU ABOUT YOUR SKINNY BRAT KIDS!

An Imagination Question for the Actor

What's your dream job?

MICHELLE THE HAIR SALON FLOOR SWEEPER

Michelle holds a broom. She's very shy but talks excitedly.

I don't have a glamorous job. I know that. Come on, I sweep the floor at a hair salon. Mostly I pick up little bits of hair. I sweep 'em all together. Long, short, blond, brown, black, all of 'em. I sweep 'em together and put them in the trash. No big deal. That's it. I'm like those guys who sweep the field at the baseball games. Or like the lady who comes out with that machine at the ice-skating place. Like that.

This job is . . . This job is . . . whatever. But you know what the fun is? The fun is when I get to hear all these women gossiping about all their husbands and their kids and who's taking who to the prom and who crashed their car and who got their house broken into. It's a very important thing, staying informed.

Some people watch the news. Me? I just mind my own business. And while I'm sweeping the floor, I'm minding everybody else's too.

An Imagination Question for the Actor

What other kind of gossip does Michelle probably hear?

MINA THE BUSINESSWOMAN

Mina is a businesswoman. She wears a suit. She hangs up a cellular phone.

I got like one minute to talk to you.

I'm supposed to do a monologue or something, but honestly? I got more important stuff to do. I have a meeting in three minutes and a phone conference at three, and you're not making my life any easier in here. My name is Mina and I do business—all kinds of business—important transactions, mortgages, re-assessments, liquidations, huge words, BIG words you wouldn't even begin to understand, so I don't know why I'm wasting my time monologuing to you.

(She checks her phone.) And on top of that I don't get any service in here.

An Imagination Question for the Actor

What kind of car does Mina drive?

MINDY THE BULLY

Mindy is the school bully. She's about to pound a kid's face in for making her look bad in class.

Listen here, Dexter. I don't know what they did at Doolin Elementary, but here, on my turf, at Dolphin Lakes Junior School, I take things kinda serious. And when I get mad, I take things into my own hands.

Now I know I'm "just a girl," but if you keep answering EVERY SINGLE QUESTION and making me look BAD in Mrs. Martin's English class, this "just a girl" is gonna become "just a fist in your lunchbox," you hear me?

I take very few things seriously. I take fighting after school seriously. I take stealing younger kids' lunch money seriously. And I take Mrs. Martin's English class seriously.

And if you keep answering when she asks us stuff about what happened in the stories we have to read for class, you're gonna make me look dumb. English is the one thing I'm good at, don't take that away from me. My fist. Your lunchbox. You like that? That was kinda like a haiku.

An Imagination Question for the Actor

What's Mindy's favorite book?

MISS MONICA, A RICH LADY WITH A TOY POODLE

Miss Monica is a fancy rich lady who just brought her toy poodle to get groomed.

Please, young man, please don't handle Tootles with such barbaric hands. She's a lady. You have to treat her like a lady.

I know she's a dog, young man, but that doesn't mean she's not a lady. I'll remind you that "lady" is a state of mind, and Tootles, my gorgeous Danish toy poodle, is more of a lady than most of the human women on this planet. And that's the truth.

I'm paying you a lot of money for your grooming services here. I expect Tootles to be treated with respect. Please only use allergen-free conditioner on her. And no coconut, she hates coconut. It makes her sneeze. Comb through each lock of her hair no more than three times. Two times leaves knots but four times damages the scalp.

Did you hear me? She's a DANISH TOY POODLE! Her breed is VERY RARE! Where did you go? YOUNG MAN?! *(She sniffs the air.)* I smell coconut! I SMELL COCONUT!

An Imagination Question for the Actor

What does Tootles look like?

NADIA THE POPSTAR FAN

Nadia sees a poster and learns the news that her favorite pop group, Tiffany and Friends, is coming in concert.

OHMYGOSH. You know what this means, Claudia? This means Tiffany and Friends are coming in concert! TIFFANY AND FRIENDS! I've been waiting for them to come in concert for years. I've been waiting to go to ANY concert—for years.

Fine. Three years, but still, it's Tiffany and Friends! I'm finally gonna be able to hear my favorite songs, live! "Love Me Like You Do," "Sweet Cherry Boy," "Sugar Meter," "Flowers on Boyfriend Row," "I'm Sorry But I Don't Like You Like That." ALL OF THEM! Agghh!!!

I'm gonna start saving up money right now. How much money do you have in your backpack? I've got seventeen cents, and that plus my lunch money today is three dollars and seventeen cents.
How much more do you think we need for concert tickets?! "TIFFANY AND FRIENDS"! Agghh!!!

An Imagination Question for the Actor

What musical act would you be excited about seeing in concert?

NATALIE THE STYLIST

Natalie chews gum and does someone's hair at her own private beauty salon.

Ay, *pobresita*. Look at you. Look at this hair. It's terrifying. It's scary. It's like a horror movie. What product are you using these days?

NO! No you're not. Bad idea. Big BAD idea, *chula*.

Why? Because anything with that much "glycerol" and "glycizerol" and whatever's gonna be a bad idea. Anything with that many chemicals is only gonna ruin the natural beauty that's going on in the natural nature of your hair.

(She calls off to her assistant, Mario.) Look at this, Mario.

(Back to her client.) You start putting chemicals in it like that, and you'll end up like Godzilla, crawling out of the sea because of too many chemicals and nuclear experiments, all crazy like a monster ready to take revenge on a whole evil world with just your hair.

Look at this texture. It's like sandpaper hair.
It's worse than sandpaper. It's like sand.

(She calls off to her assistant, Mario.) Mario, cancel all my appointments and get me hair protein, this is gonna run a little longer than expected.

An Imagination Question for the Actor

What does sandpaper hair feel like?

NICKY THE CHORUS GIRL

Nicky is a fifth-grader in a chorus class. Her teacher sends her to a special room to warm up. She sings some bad notes, then someone interrupts her.

You can't come in here. I'm doing my vocal warm-ups. Don't interrupt me. It's all very technical, all this stuff. Vocal stuff. Vocal-cord stuff. Throat coating and all that jazz. Ha, ha. "All that jazz." That's a music term. We musicians have a bunch of terms we use, and we throw 'em around like that.

I SAID you can't come in here! Do you want me to call Mr. Flores the chorus teacher? He'll tell you that I need to warm up. He sends me in here during chorus class to warm up because he says my vocal cords need extraspecial attention, and this soundproof room is the only place where I can truly get a full-bodied warm-up.

What do you mean he just "doesn't wanna hear" me?

An Imagination Question for the Actor

Is Nicky a good singer?

OFELIA THE DOG WALKER

Ofelia holds four or five leashes. Four or five dogs are tugging her every which way. She's a dog walker.

Fifi, get back here. Bruno, watch it. Don't sniff that. That's garbage. Krispy, don't step in that. You're gonna get your paws dirty. Chewie! CHEWIE!

Why couldn't I be a librarian? Or work in a video store or something? Or even a restaurant? Why did I have to decide I wanted to be a dog walker? It's just not smart.

Freddy, don't bite him. He didn't bite you. Bruno, say you're sorry.

At least at a restaurant or a library I'd be able to work with people, with real live PEOPLE. Not like this. Here they just—FIFI! FIFI, get away from that! It'S NASTY!—People don't sniff garbage. Or get tangled all in each other's leashes. Or bite each other.

KRISPY, don't you dare get near that puddle!

A Hidden-Clue Question for the Actor

How many dogs is Ofelia walking?

PALOMA THE PIGEON

Paloma is a pigeon.

I spend my life in the park. Can you imagine that? No, you can't. 'Cause you're too busy working and doing homework and getting on the subway and driving around and shopping at the mall.

Not me. My whole life: the park. Sometimes older people come and throw me old popcorn, and I eat it, or I don't, depends on what kind of mood I'm in. Then I go back up and chill on a tree or maybe on a statue or a monument, and I do whatever I want, wherever I want.

I fly. Just coast around. Tree to tree. Building to building. But it all comes back to one place . . . It all comes back to the green grass and the dogs walking and the kids on skateboards at the park. Such is the life of a pigeon.

Spanish form? *Paloma*. And my life? Rocks.

An Imagination Question for the Actor

What other things do pigeons do?

TIA PAOLA

Tia Paola is that aunt that you're afraid to see at parties because she makes you feel so awkward. Here's one reason why.

Ay pero look at you! You need to gain some weight! *Estas SUPER-flaca!* You look like your mother did when she came over from Colombia! I can see your ribs! I can see your bones. You're all *huesos*. You look sick! You need hips! Look at me! I'm all hips! You need that!

Isn't there a Burger King like right next to your mother's house? Don't you like chocolate milkshakes? We need to get some of those in you. We need to fatten you up. If not, no one's ever gonna marry you.

I know you're only ten, but still . . . it's never too early to start worrying!

An Imagination Question for the Actor

What kind of car does Tia Paola drive?

PERLA THE CHECKOUT COUNTER LADY

Perla works behind the counter at a grocery store. She wears an apron and a badge with her name on it.

(Perla scans someone's groceries. She looks at the food they're buying.) Is this good? This cereal? *Los* Krispy Krunchies? My kids want me to buy them, I'm not sure. Too much sugar, I think . . . and you don't wanna give MY kids sugar. They go crazy. Really crazy. They dropped the TV from the fire escape the other day just because they "wanted to see what was inside"! I told them, I said, "You wanna know what's inside? What's inside is, you're grounded!" That's what I said. Hah.

(She scans more groceries.) Ay, look at this. I hadn't seen this before. Is this new? I didn't know we had this flavor.

(She scans some more groceries, finishes. The customer moves to pay.) Cash or card? Ay, I like your nails. Credit or debit? My sister has an account at the same bank. Enter your PIN number. I'm not supposed to look . . . Cash back?

Thank you for coming. See you tomorrow. Tell me how the Krispy Krunchies work out for you. Hide your TV.

A Hidden-Clue Question for the Actor

Why does Perla tell the customer to hide the TV?

PILAR THE MERMAID

Pilar is a mermaid. She seems annoyed.

Pay no attention to the stuff you've seen in movies. Being a mermaid is not cute. We don't normally sing on rocks in the morning. We aren't friends with crabs and lobsters and fish and seagulls. As a matter of fact, crabs look funny, lobsters creep me out, fish smell bad, and seagulls make just about the most annoying noises you could ever imagine.

Oh, and most importantly: Men really don't fall in love with us. They don't go, "Oh, look at that, a beautiful mermaid. I must be in love." You know what they do? They go, "Oh my gosh, look at that, bro!," and they get their camera phones and their video cameras and they videotape us and put it on YouTube. They catch us in nets and try to put us on display in freak shows and run us over on jet skis and speedboats.

And no, I don't have gorgeous flowing red hair. No one I know has gorgeous flowing red hair. We live in SALTwater. You know what that means? Have you ever heard of SPLIT ENDS?

An Imagination Question for the Actor

What would be some of the cool things about being a mermaid?

PIOLA THE LOUSE

Piola is a louse. In Spanish, the word for "lice" is piojos.

I am a louse. I am a louse bug. I will attack your scalp, jump on your head from another person's head while you're on the bus . . . Or maybe you'll share a hat or a comb or a something . . . and from there in, it's ALL OVER.

(An evil laugh.) HA, HA, HA, HA, HA. I'll burrow and dig deep into your pretty curls, and I'll make screechy noises like "KAAAAAH!" to signal to my louse bug friends to come join me.

(An evil laugh.) HA, HA, HA, HA, HA. We'll lay eggs and have a party and maybe play Monopoly in your head while you sleep, while you're at school, and the only way to get rid of us is to use weird shampoo chemicals that smell like vinegar and salad dressing.

(An evil laugh.) HA, HA, HA, HA, HA. My name is Piola. I'm a *piojo*. I am a louse. HEAR ME ROAR.

A Hidden-Clue Question for the Actor

How can people avoid getting lice?

SANDY THE DOG

Sandy is frustrated with her owner.

My owner buys me the silliest stuff. The other day, he bought me this little furry toy thing that he thinks is so cool. It looks like a gerbil or something, and it makes this AWFUL squeaky noise, and he squeezes it, and it goes "SQUEEEEEEAK," and then he throws it, and I go and I catch it and I bring it back to him, and I'm trying to tell him—I mean, I'm a dog, but we communicate in our own special ways—and I'm trying to tell him, "Dude, go return this. This toy stinks," but he insists on throwing it again, and he keeps saying the word "fetch," and I don't know what that means, but as soon as he's said it, he's thrown it again . . .

And I get it, and I bring it back, and I'm like "DUDE, RETURN THIS," but he throws it again, and about three hours later, I'm so tired from trying to get him to return this ugly stupid gerbil toy that I just fall asleep.

A Hidden-Clue Question for the Actor

What game is the owner playing with the dog?

SOFIA THE SLACKER

Sofia tries to explain why she'd rather watch TV than do homework.

It's not that I don't do homework. It's not that I don't like school—I do—it's just that I always, somehow, end up putting everything off to the last minute. I know I shouldn't, but I can't help it. The world is a busy and wonderful place, and I can't help it if I want to enjoy every second of it.

Last year, I had to do a science project. It was due on a Tuesday. Unfortunately, it was due on the Tuesday right around the finals on *American Popstar Showcase.*

What's a girl supposed to do?! You can't give up finding out who the next American popstar is just to do homework! A science project? Are you kidding me? Who cares about volcanoes and spore molds and "which detergent works the best"?! All I wanna know is Reggie gonna beat out Stacy and is Sabrina gonna make it to the final four!

A Hidden-Clue Question for the Actor

What day of the week was the Science Project due?

SOL

Sol is the sun. Or maybe she's a little girl playing pretend.

No life on earth would exist without me. I am the light and the warmth of the whole entire world. I am the sun.

I know it might seem a little crazy but trust me.

You don't have telescopes powerful enough to see me yet. The light is THAT strong. Your best scientists can only imagine what I look like deep down inside. They will spend the next five hundred years building spaceships and satellites and astro-cameras to take pictures of my insides.

But trust me. I'm telling you. This is what I look like. A little Hispanic girl who is barely ten years old.

The planets revolve around me. I am the sun.

An Imagination Question for the Actor

What do you imagine the inside of the sun to look like?

VANESSA THE CELL PHONE STORE GIRL

Vanessa is trying to sell you a cell phone.

We have many many packages with many options. This is the new TW-3400 phone. It has a built-in camera—that's a new feature. The TW-3500 brings a built-in camera PLUS a tape deck, but for starters, I recommend the TW-3400 just in case you don't want to, you know, go over budget.

We have carrying cases and accessories over here. You're probably going to need to buy a clear case, a leather case, a belt-loop connector, a car charger, a home charger, an airplane charger—I know it sounds crazy, but I use mine all the time. And also, if you're smart, you'll get an extended superwarranty package, just in case your phone falls into the toilet.

An Imagination Question for the Actor

What other "cellular phone accessories" can you think up?

VIOLETA THE MEXICAN PENGUIN

Violeta is the world's first Mexican penguin.

Hi. My name is Violeta. I was born in Mexico. And I'm a penguin.

Being the world's first Mexican penguin wasn't a big shock to me. I was born in a zoo, my parents were both from Alaska, they looked just like me, we ate fish—no big deal.

But the whole world went crazy! There was a newspaper clipping taped to the door of my little ice room at the Mexico City zoo when I was a baby. It read, "World's First Mexican Penguin," and I had to see it every day. It was a constant reminder that I was different, and at first, it kinda bothered me, but after a while, I thought it was kinda cool.

All the other penguins were talking about Alaska and seals and glaciers and ice stuff, and I was just like "*Odale, pinguinos*," and that made me special.

A Hidden-Clue Question for the Actor

Where was Violeta born?

YENNISE THE SHOPA-HOLIC

Yennise holds about ten or twenty shopping bags.

I have a problem. I admit it. I do. I have a shopping problem, and I need to stop, but it's not that easy. It's never really easy, because, well, they had a sale. A GOOD SALE. It was two-for-one at Tracy's, and I had a twenty percent off coupon for Middleton's, and Georgie needed shirts, so I got him a couple at Shirt-Mart and . . . well . . . credit cards make it so easy.

They do. You just swipe and you sign, and it's like there was no money exchanged, none at all. And you don't even realize how much you've bought until you got home, and you realize you need to make two or three trips to the car to get all the stuff you bought.

So I'm sorry. I know I need help with my problem, but right now, I need help bringing stuff into the house. There's more in the trunk.

An Imagination Question for the Actor

What stores would you like to shop in?

ZARA THE LATIN SOAP STAR

Zara is a very beautiful star on Telenovelas, *Latin soap operas. Everything about her is very dramatic.*

I've been an actress since I was very young, but it wasn't until I turned twelve that I realized what I really REALLY wanted to do. I was born to be on *Telenovelas*. I remember seeing my first *Telenovela* on my abuelo's television set in the living room. Everyone was so beautiful, everyone was so . . . dramatic.

The music was wonderful and the cameras zoomed in on people's faces when they said things like, *"No, Mario, nunca mas,"* or, *"No es hijo, es tu hijo!"*

I didn't even speak very good Spanish at the time; I still don't. But I've been on five *Telenovelas* in the last ten years. I had starring roles in three of them.

All I have to do is work on my acting faces. I have "shocked." *(She makes a shocked face.)* And "scared." *(She makes a scared face.)* And "You stole all my money and my husband and now I'm going to ruin your wedding." *(She makes THAT face.)*

A Hidden-Clue Question for the Actor

How many Telenovelas has Zara been on?

ABOUT THE AUTHOR

M. Ramirez is a Miami native and a graduate of NYU's Dramatic Writing program. His monologues and scenes for young actors have won Critic's Choice Awards at Thespian Society Competitions at district, state, and national levels. He is a two-time winner of the Latino Playwriting Award from the Kennedy Center's American College Theater Festival. His plays have been produced at FringeNYC, the Mad Cat Theatre Company, City Theatre's Summer Shorts, and Actors Theatre of Louisville.